a theory of everything

a theory of everything

MARY CROCKETT HILL

Autumn House Press

PITTSBURGH

"Autumn House" and "Autumn House Press" are registered trademarks owned by Autumn House Press, a nonprofit corporation whose mission is the publication and promotion of poetry and other fine literature.

Autumn House Press Staff
Executive Editor and Founder: Michael Simms
Executive Director: Richard St. John
Community Outreach Director: Michael Wurster
Co-Director: Eva-Maria Simms
Fiction Editor: Sharon Dilworth
Coal Hill Editor: Joshua Storey
Associate Editors: Anna Catone, Laurie Mansell Reich, Rebecca Clever, Philip Terman
Assistant Editor: Bernadette James
Editorial Consultant: Ziggy Edwards
Media Consultant: Jan Beatty
Tech Crew Chief: Michael Milberger
Interns: Carolyne Whelan, Laura Vrcek

ISBN: 978-1-932870-27-5

for
Isabelle, Samson, Crockett
and of course Stewart

■

my everythings

Contents

■ in spite of everything

■ the end of everything

Acknowledgments

Bellingham Review, "February"
Boxcar Poetry Review, "A Novel About a Glass of Water"
Dislocate, "Pantoum for Attachment"
Gargoyle, "My Sister the Buddhist Prays with the Fleas,"
  "Toaster Genesis"
Juked, "Newton's Cradle," "This Is the World"
Miranda, "The Photographer," "Swan"
New Delta Review, "The Lost Child, Her Step-brother, the
  Neighbor, the Pastor, the Person of Interest"
New Letters, "Woodbridge"
Night Train, "Alien Wedding," "The Fat Cat"
Pank, "Why I Gave Up On Astral Projection"
Pebble Lake Review, "Poem for What Has Come"
Rhino, "A Theory of Everything"
Rio, "Sky" (formerly named "This")
Rock & Sling, "The Little Girls"
Salt Flats Annual, "The Museum of Weightlessness," "Wes"
Snow Monkey, "Cupboard"
Tipton Poetry Journal, "All About It," "Finding Good"
The Tusculum Review, "I Ching"
Whistling Shade, "Young People Today"

Thanks to Melanie Almeder, Bonnie Soniat, Jon Musgrove, Jessie Graybill, Maurice Ferguson, Polly Pauley, Rick Trethewey, Nick Regiacorte, Jenny Bitner, Beth Wellington, Adrian Blevins, Cynthia Atkins, Amanda Cockrell, James Broschart, Bob Hicok, and Mike Simms for their insights. Thanks also to the Roanoke College English Department and William E. Keister Endowment for the support that made this book possible. Thanks to my mother, father, brothers, sisters, and in-laws for giving me lots of good company, food, and stories. And finally, thanks to my husband and children for loving me especially when I don't deserve it.

a theory of everything

According to string theory, which is our best hope
of uniting General Relativity and Quantum Theory
into a Theory of Everything, space-time ought to have
ten dimensions, not just the four that we
experience. The idea is that six of these ten
dimensions are curled up into a space so small,
that we don't notice them.

"Space and Time Warps"
Public Lecture
Stephen W. Hawking

■ A Theory of Everything

It has something to do with invisible string
rippling out across a universal sunset,
wrapping us up like the perfect brown corded package.

Something to do with the vibration of stars—
how they flicker in tune with each other, humming cosmically.
And though I've never seen this reported anywhere

I also believe it has something to do with dogs.
For who else has such capacity to forgive
an entirely other species? Well, yes, God

but I don't mess around with God.
So in my theory, the wet nose of a dog
fits in the space where our heart has been cut out.

And after dogs, the pure yellow of lemons,
the affection small children hold for Band-aids, the urge
to touch a stranger's bald head.

It all has a place in the Theory.
Name it and I will hang it on the clothesline.
Name it, I will chop it up for soup.

What's not to believe, anyway, in a theory
that has room enough for all other theories,
even those that say this Theory is shit?

Sure, the vibration of strings we cannot measure.
And yes, the strings are so fine we haven't
found them yet. One might surmise

this is not about strings, but our desire
for strings. You too are welcome
at this Party of Everything.

Come to my house where
we will speak of aqueducts and whiskers,
we will eat brown bread and touch our feet

under the table. You can tell me
we are not connected, that there is nothing
holding us together.

I will tug your ear and peck you softly on the lips.

everything before us

We had everything before us,
we had nothing before us....

A Tale of Two Cities
Charles Dickens

■ This Is the World

This is also the world.
A small boy drops
a maple leaf down a well.
A girl, slightly larger, does likewise—
peering over the stone lip to guess
the leaf's curled and wayward descent.

Across the yard, behind a stardust bush,
the housecat is toying with something still alive.
It flits through the grass, now here now there,
delighting the cat with its antic struggle for flight.

I am in the world too, wondering:
Do I kill the bird for mercy? Do I take it inside?
What would Dickon from *The Secret Garden* do?
The book-animals loved him so, showing their mildest
bellies beneath satisfied, glinting eyes.

I might think we all want such love,
even from a half-dead bird—except
my brother was once chased down a walking trail
by a man who'd just killed his first turkey
and to celebrate, downed three six-packs
and started firing at hikers. He hounded after
my brother, hollering for all the world
like Yosemite Sam, "I'm gonna get you, I'll get you!"

The man later told the police, "It seemed at the time
like the thing to do."

This is the world,
                    and where we spit,
where we stomp, where we fuck and crap,
and all that Jack built, and whatever's next,
and whether we forgive our father
or trust strangers or take zoloft,
and why the trees on one side of the hill
bud green before the others,
and if we make our way to Egypt,

and who there holds a broom, and who a gun,
and once we finally lie down at the end of the day
on our mattress or hammock or stone slab,
how the moon just keeps throbbing
so we sense loss too keenly,
and what finally *is* the thing to do—
      and if we carry our children
            inside our own bodies, and where
      we plant our pumpkin seeds,
and why we fear caves
and dark
      underwater places,
the dark under water,
the dark
      —someone please stop me,
I could go on forever, it is
after all, the world.

■ Swan

You are beautiful in a way that is also animal—
a swan, damp and muscled, throbs in your neck.

Your hand, the blank of pure butter, is taut with potential
Other—the ripple of knuckles like imagined flight.

It is easy to envision feathers,
fine tender bones, the tuft of bird down.

More than ever, I want to sit in a concert hall
where music is made from heartbeats:

people all over the globe, monitored for pulse
(people frying onions, masturbating, nursing babies, people

sighing as they rustle paper or furtively scratch their behinds)
each with a cord attached to the heart

and on the other end, a cellphone sending signals
to a cable in a shiny bucket of water.

It is art, but I do not expect it to save us.
Even the most magnificent notions can be turned into a dirty joke.

You and I in our animal skins, crossing the market, our pockets
bulging with tart yellow apples, three in each hand.

Even so, I look up to find sky above us—
sky and what comes with it,

the urge to raise my arms
and drift upward into blue.

■ All About It

He looked like sullied laundry, which is to say
Jeff Clark, which is to say the scrubby field
where Jeff Clark took me when I was 5 and he 13
to teach me, as he put it, how to hump.

Jeff didn't take my clothes off, or his for that matter,
or stick any one of his parts into any one of mine.
He just led me out into the first light of November
where even I suspected we should not have come.

He said, "I bet you don't know anything," and I told him
"I know all about it," and he said, "Show me then."
So I did to him what my brother had described.
It must have looked ridiculous — this thin-boned child

in wrinkled corduroys and mittens, pumping
her intrepid hips against the dawn of 1975.
Perhaps it is wrong for me to smile when thinking on it.
But it is my memory. I'll do with it what I want.

■ Alien Wedding

You send me a card
that says you are marrying an alien
next Sunday—a week before Thanksgiving
in the Year of Our Lord Two Thousand Eight.

A spaceship hovers
over a brooding church.

Jenny Bitner
&
IG9
invite you to share with them
the joy of their marriage.

And I have to wonder, is this about turning thirty?

Are you trying to reclaim your menstrual dream:
Hermes on a Harley, rubbing hot thighs—
the drive toward birth tents and underwater voodoo?

True, it was a ride any woman
would envy: you were opened wide
by a messenger, a god—all the while
the engine purred & ripped you
forward into space.

Now you're thirty and something has to happen;
it might as well be this.
You stand in a simple tulle dress, small cream shoes
like pastries on your feet.
Beside you, your roommate as channeler
for the beloved, elusive IG9, holds your hand
and vows eternities.

But what if that roommate
feels no IG9 within her, no moment
of melting, of liquid skoal, no pinball
chime and whirr?

What if that hazy yellow dot
at the horizon/in your periphery/on the table/under the table
is a blemish on your eyeball?
Not a vision, not a visitation.

And the sky, quite blue—
                              vacant
of all but a semi-colon cloud—
the hushed sky watches
as no one arrives.

■ Sky

Not unthought of, exactly, but a blind inside knowing
like the wind's fist knows the gnarled hollow of valley
where cypress sprouts unheeding out of rock
—and we're under the cypress, on the rock,
wearing the brown cloaks of a time before opera, and yet hear
the gothic strain of it swirl around our heads.
We are in the valley, still uncertain what it is
keeping us grounded, keeping us from
reeling into the wild.

■ History

You ask, *Does it matter?*—And yes,
it always mattered. After all, the roads
    came from somewhere, didn't they?
Roads I could never engineer as I am no
    passing buffalo or even handy with a rake.
These roads, astounding, lead anywhere
    and then again, they will go right back
to the place they started. So without history,
    we'd be stuck in an overgrown field
with no lawn mower, much less the cotton gin;
    without it, we'd be hunching down
to tug the teats of cows.
                I suppose we might
    observe the beasts, do what they do:
find the warm side of a hill, sip
    from the river, sleep propped up
against a willow trunk and cow-dream
    the earth as it should have been—
a land of eyeglasses and bridges
    and mathematical equations scribbled
on chalkboards, ribbons spun
    from the bellies of worms—
I'd dream myself held up, suspended
    like a pop-up ballerina in a child's jewelry box
by the twirl of all that has passed and is passing,
    a miniature self with her pink plastic toe on the brink,
spinning away toward that moment
    in the distant pasture of tomorrow
when flying nuns and bruised peaches
    will be equally cherished, equally so.

too much everything

too much smoke – too much noise –
too much houses – too much men –
too much every thing

Two unidentified Eskimos,
when asked their impressions of London,
quoted in Maria Edgeworth's
Practical Education, 1835

■ Woodbridge

Peepfrogs going off like sirens
in the field that will not long be a field.

Three bulldozers this week, a portajohn, a freshly graveled road.

In the brown past dusk, the huge metal tube
that will funnel sewage
has such romance in its silver
it seems a passage
to something exceedingly rare:
a spiraling light
or colony of thumb-sized trolls.

With rain, with spring, with the seed
of a new child in my womb, I am better prepared
to lose this pasture that was never mine.

Twenty-six tidy new houses—full of the stuff that fills houses,
the La-Z-Boys and breakfast stools and liquid soap—
will sit there and there, where the cows bleated and roamed,
where my teenage boyfriend groped me one chilled night,
oblivious to the damp of our toes.

There was always the cow pasture, always the option
of walking westward through the fields
into unnamed mountains beyond.

Even if we never walked it. Even if we just stayed home.

■ Wes

You might think this is all about loss, wanting
her shoulder as it turns to the wall, her dimming eye,
drumming finger tip. There's something inside that assures you,
    heaven
will contain everyone you love in a single lush landscape—
maybe a meadow tinged with porcelain light, a dusty lemon tree;
there in that gymnasium of cloud and harp music, everyone
    intimate, everyone family.

You know better. The people you love leave town,
go crazy on drugs, keep talking about religion, stop loving you
    back.
And now this girl—even when she walks down the same hallways,
sits two tables away at lunch, munching green beans—is not
    yours anymore.

She had promised everything one might expect: never to wash
    herself
after you touched her, to taste you like a sermon on her skin.
So how can it be she dumped you after swearing her love?

It's not good to think too much about having, Wes—
though the old man who comes to the museum where I work
keeps telling me that he and I both have it all.
Yesterday I visited his long brick ranch
near the highway north of town
to pick up a chunk of the original White House
from his days in the secret service under Truman.

He ushered me into the dank-smelling Florida room
and proclaimed, "We have everything here. Look at this,
three acres and a creek, the pet cemetery
out back, a pretty spot for picnics."

An indoor rock garden had been stocked
with plush teddy bears wearing Santa hats, huge
stuffed frogs, and plastic poinsettias in hanging wicker baskets.
He made me look in every room: the paintings by Eisenhower,

sturdy kitchen cabinets, a step machine, and this rarity
—a decorative teak chair from "the place where people worship
  monkeys"
that took two men, he said, an entire lifetime to carve.

The next morning, I arrive late to work, my hair unbrushed
and coca-cola splattered down the lap of my jeans;
he is waiting in the driveway. He has another piece—
a better piece—of the White House
that he wants to trade me for my small, cracked chunk.

The first words he utters upon entering the museum basement,
before even the lights are turned on:
"You have everything here. Everything."
And I can't help thinking, *what in the world could he mean?*

■ The Fat Cat

If you happen upon an immensely fat cat on the road
don't ask what he's been eating as he just might tell you
this gruesome litany: his gruel and the pot and the old lady too
five birds in a flock and seven girls dancing and the lady with the
  pink parasol
Red Hottentot Tony Jowls Jerry Flop and on and on until he names
  you—
and then, friend, you are in the belly of a cat
where no one can reach you without the aid of an ax.

It is the same for the over-age skateboarders outside the Dollar
  General.
When they call, *Hey Cuz... Hello?... keep walking.*

And that stricken man dressed in a monk-frock and lugging
a stuffed duffle bag onto the bus, under no circumstance
strike up a conversation. Yes, there is what seems to be
a toy light saber poking out from the broken zipper of his bag.
Yes, a surge protector. A wooden pan-flute.
A dingy inflatable doll of Dora the Explorer.
Stop looking, just stop looking. Still,

how can we help but love him with our God-bless-the-crazies love
that wants to hold his thin, veined hand and say, *let's have some
  soup.*

But is soup certifiably safe? Will the monk-wanna-be
stand below the apartment window with a boom-box
blasting European techno-ballads and throwing rocks?
He'll phone from the Orange Market down the corner
to say he's strangled two pigeons for dinner—
to say the inside of his mouth
has molted its muscular husk.

Someone should write a manual for avoiding random horrors.
Someone needs to tell me what to do with these birds.

■ Jars

There are many ways to fill them, so much
on this side of sanity that must be kept.

Buttons, of course you think of buttons,
coins, Q-tips, bolts, wads of string,

but have you given thought
to what should not be preserved?

My brother Sam, for example, would fart
his rankest disappointments

into an empty mayonnaise jar
and keep it on the mantle

until we young ones returned.
"Edgar, I have something for you,"

he'd almost sing. A flying headbutt,
a body slam, and Edgar

was pinned to the floor, his nose
mashed into the open mouth of glass.

Also this: tiny sharks, dismembered fingers,
unborn anythings: all the bloated

wonders on a laboratory shelf.
If I were a better person I might say love

should never be contained
but forgiveness must be kept jarred

on your bedside table where you could find it
even when you wished you could not.

I am not that person. I am the one
who thinks of toenail clippings and lard,

peaches waxing bluish-brown,
the body-juice of bees.

Is it possible that toenails equal love?
Lard, forgiveness?

Might the million jars of our world
choreograph their own end—

wrenching themselves open at the same
exact moment to spew their contents in a whirled

rebellion, the air flocked with all the things
we should have thrown away?

I've been told Pandora's box
was really a jar, and she herself

made of earth and water, a jar
full of the need to open

what the gods had given her—
plague, sorrow, poverty

of mind, and the hope
that what was to come

could be both binding
and boundless.

■ The Photographer

It's really a matter of looking up everyday.
Eventually, the clouds will reveal
amazing substance: all 26 letters of the alphabet, for example,
the numbers 0-9, white wisps against eternal blue—
the word "splat" or the King James version of the Bible, one letter
    at a time,
enough to count infinity, enough to write
"more copulation!" or "pink sheets" in cloud letters
as if ordained by the sky.
This can happen in a town where nothing of import has occurred
since King Cola went out of business in 1935.

Two years, anywhere, and a patient camera.
Language will unfurl.

And so the idea that we could be silent, while sweet, is truly not
    convincing.
Even the radio spokeswoman for catholic hermits in West Virginia
quotes them as saying *something*.

Elsewhere at this hour geese are sprawling
                                fernlike across the firmament.
Their words are not important to us perhaps,
                        but surely they are speaking.

Wings in light.

■ Wings

If the geese in your mind are not white, not gray
not afraid of any other goose
as they soar in their own undeniably rosy glow—

well, that is your passion, of course, straining madly toward the spot
where the one you love propped you
for a right honorable bang the night before.

But here it turns complex, for you and beloved make babies.
And the love for babies is a stout brown goose rife with worry.
Windows are suddenly something to fear

and men dressed like Santa, whom we tell our pliant offspring
are indeed only men dressed like Santa
so they will not wander (believing in goodness) away with some
    pervert in a red suit.

Ditto sheriffs. Ditto tailors and monks and electricians and teachers
and those who lose dogs in the park. *Oh please.*
Can't we be the good children who place apples in the derelict's
    hands?

Must we flap our way windward—feathers
whirling like confetti, always muscle, always straining, always
honk, honk, honk, honk?

everything, lost

She has known everything, borne and suffered
everything, lost everything and shed her last tear.

Les Misérables
Victor Hugo

■ Why I Gave Up On Astral Projection

My body, when was it
I realized you are so full
of shit? Literally. Shit.

The food and the churnings
—all the blood-heavy
mass of you. The old binding

between us, now fixed.
There was a time I did not know
I even had a body.

I was all in my head,
nouns vibrating
like tiny harps.

It seemed inevitable to float
above those organs, that skin,
so likely at any moment to slip

from my supine shell
and surge into the universe.
(I dreamed I could leave

then come back.
Will such faith also return?
The whiskered self

shaved clean again
by the cutting ache
for flight.) There is a blue cord

holding me back. And more—
the children, the child in me
who now knows what she eats,

my neighbor's dying lover, his rickety
lawn chair, the bend of my mouth saying no,
the waiting, the laundry, the need

to spoon and stir in a room
that will not be the moon
no matter, no matter how I worship it.

■ Newton's Cradle

I was once a child on a trampoline
with my friend Mary
and me also Mary—
we two like the persistent
knock and bob
of that metal-balls motion toy
that rich men keep idle
on their desks. We were
so glad for our long girl legs,
bruised knee-caps, mane-ish hair,
for the all of us that sprung
and jounced and all but flew
from taut black canvas
below. So glad
that no one had yet
kissed us, much less
fingered, much less photographed
naked. We were anything
but still, and the air
was not moving
but seemed to be moving
because we shot through it so fast.

■ The Little Girls

How they must have loved the flowers—
generations of pink and lavender
in his small side yard, the careless
abundance of orange. I had seen it
from the road and, with a grain of envy,
wondered at the life that could nurture
such a garden. Now I see the blossoms
were not an offering to the birds.

And the old man who tended them
—in an airless jail cell now
hurling his head again and again
against the metal bed frame
so that his skull might crack
and release the ochre inside.

Let it go—with it, the thought
of him taking her little fingers
and guiding them to his prick,
the blue walls of the pool house,
the white walls of the church,
the round bellies, narrow hips,
breastless nipples he would press
his palms against as if to keep them small.

Let go his wordless boots,
the dust of chalk
haloing his fingers, that barricaded
school room door—
it must all go, but where
could we possibly put such things?

I want to say the meadow.
I want to think there are plants
that could breathe in what would kill us
and breathe out oxygen,

—and there, the blurred voices,
the grimacing fingers,
the horrible, horrible needs
turn still for a moment, calm

and the little girls
can walk in the grass
without recalling so much
as the waxy scrawl
of a crayon, the fold of a collar
or pulse of a breath.

■ Pantoum for Attachment

My sister the Buddhist says it's my problem.
I say it makes sense I don't want to let go
the hand of my daughter as she sleeps this morning
in the bare room, or the bare room itself for that matter.

I say it makes sense I don't want to let go
—the worn rug, the coffee mug left on the mantle
in the bare room, or the bare room itself for that matter,
the million invisible atoms we're breathing,

the worn rug, the coffee mug left on the mantle,
the half-lit smile she'll make when I wake her,
the million invisible atoms we're breathing—
I want it, of course, I want this touch to become

the half-lit smile she'll make when I wake her,
the nutshell of her small brown head.
I want it, of course, I want this touch to become
enough for the rest of whatever is coming.

The nutshell of her small brown head
turns in her sleep like agreement, cunning
enough for the rest of whatever is coming.
A bird cries morning. Watch as she

turns in her sleep like agreement, cunning,
into a woman in a raincoat by the side of the road.
A bird cries. Morning. Watch as she
(anyone, not my daughter, this other, this vision

of a woman in a raincoat by the side of the road)
walks under the sky as if it were breathing.
Anyone, not my daughter, this other, this vision
I must, my sister says, release. She

walks under the sky as if it were breathing
in all the loose thoughts of a collective sun.
I must, my sister says, release. She
doesn't understand. Why should I let go?

In all the loose thoughts of a collective sun,
where lies the love my grasping mother-love
doesn't understand? Why should I let go
of her tender-boned, still small hand

where lies the love my grasping mother-love
builds a nest to rest in? I would make a sculpture
of her tender-boned, still small hand
—a totem to carry against the future,

a nest to rest in. I would make a sculpture—
the hand of my daughter as she sleeps into morning,
a totem to carry against the future.
My sister the Buddhist says it's my problem.

■ The Lost Child, Her Step-brother, the Neighbor, the Pastor, the Person of Interest

There is something like a tree, but greener, softer, griefless,
where the tortured find a bed.
And the sky, made up of the endlessness of being
a mother to children who may at any time
jump off a roof, get mauled by roving dogs
or forced down a ladder
—the sky is not their problem.

Likewise, the centuries we spent painting
glorious pictures of Jesus and his mother, such exuberant
tumbles of cloth, hair, all those difficult hands,
just to find ourselves here, A-10 of the *Roanoke Times & World
News*
where all—*not their problem, not their problem.*

My friend Mary was obsessed with Jesus.
I think she took it personally, her name
as calling. Would it be any easier for her to have children?
And yet Mary of the paintings seems to know what's in store.
Even with the chubby sweet air of Godchild hovering,
she has these far-off eyes.

In the Dear Annie advice column (Extra, page 6)
a woman asks what she's supposed to do
about her son who killed someone.
I find it hard to go on living when I think of that poor girl.
Let's tell the lady that the girl is now unburdened — voiceless
limbs
cradle her green slumber... and above, a speckled bird
holds whatever she's forgotten in the dusk of his ruby red throat.

■ Oh the Dreadful

Wind and rain. Again, the question
of whether we can bend our violence
into music—the drowned sister's breastbone
fashioned as a clumsy violin,
long hairs plucked for the bow.

It is love, of course, in a maudlin folk tune,
but in life, more likely pornography.
Have you noticed the way mass-murderers
are always described by the strippers
they hired weeks before?

There is the credit card receipt,
the computer screen flaring
with downloaded lips, tits, crotches.
"He creeped me out," the women invariably say.
"Like he already knew what he wanted to do."

On my part, there is suspicion
that putting these words in a line
one after another
edges them toward
the hymnal.

But what I least want is music.

What I cannot believe is anything
beautiful, swanlike, lyric.

Oh poem, kindly go away.
Leave me and my paper alone.

in spite of everything

In spite of everything, I still believe that people
are really good at heart.

Anne Frank
Diary
July 15, 1944

■ I Ching

Above the lake is fire.
Above heaven, also fire.
Above the fire, flame.

Two sisters who have walked side by side their whole lives
diverge.

On account of fire, I cannot wake my baby to my breast.
For fire, I feel a question stirring.
Under fire, I am the body of the second sister, heading west.

Is desire born out of lack, or has it always been there,
having nothing to do with need?

A radical change is at hand. Fire.
A contradiction seizes your throat.
On the island of people who hate you, you will find a friend.

Blessings enter through the eye.

Go to that island. Stretch your hands
up to the womb-side of the earth.

The place you didn't expect to still be there.

■ Young People Today

Apparently they're having sex and eating
non-stop Taco Bell and wearing strange
perfumes and t-shirts that proclaim,
"Hey you! Wanna have my baby?"

And I've considered it and yes I do.
I want that blind white tug
of baby mouth, the pull of milk
as ostentatious as the high note

that a diva won't stop singing.
Looking back, I want more
of sun and field and blanket,
the groundhog who is always

twenty feet away, gnawing
yard greens and pretending
he doesn't see me
so he won't have to run.

In the sense that all pleasures
are at root a threat, I want
a ship that sails into oblivion,
its curtains warbling *tra-la, tra-lee*

and the mercy of horizons
beyond reach. I should stop
to ask what you want.
What is it? Surely

not my baby after all.
I might guess something
between possession and longing
—a folded sheet of paper

made gauzy by the lamplight,
but that would just be
guessing. Instead, let's do this:
hold the quiet of my hand

as we sit and watch the weather
tumble into evening. Perhaps
you'll take out your spent chewing gum
and loll it between your fingers.

Perhaps the sky will open
clamorous petals above us
and what I don't want to look at
will blur in its descent.

■ For Stinky in the Rockies

I read of your problem in the paper, dear Stinky,
and of the many who want you to know
you are not alone. We all stink sometimes. It is only
the film on your scalp and toes, possibly your rear,
writes one reader from Minnesota: You must scour
these places daily with a rough rag, spumy with soap.

Not so, says Chicago. It's too simple: Just a pill of zinc
and your troubles will melt like buttermint on the tongue.

Oddly, John R. Myers, M.D., of Siler City, North Carolina,
insists that your smell is *musky*, not, as you call it, *musty*
and it comes from oil-producing glands in your skin.
He writes—how like a doctor—*There is nothing you can do.*

And California—how like a Californian—contends your odor
stems from the kind of systemic physiological imbalance
that Western medicine rarely addresses.

From New York: The culprit is dampness. Men need
to throw away their sweat-soaked belts and start fresh more often.
From Down South: Do you have an old smelly dog that sleeps on
   your couch?

Wisconsin has been listening to talk radio. South Texas
is an expert deer hunter. They have notions of their own
   regarding stink:
alcohol, corn starch, acupuncture, selenium sulfide shampoo,
more protein, less fat, a vegan diet, running
the hot water tap before you launder your clothes.

There are so many keys to that single scent-free garden door
where ladies twirl white parasols as they stroll,
albino peacocks pecking at their feet.

Yet, how could I want you to live there, Stinky, dear friend,
for there is something so comforting in stink.

My mother's garlic/onion regimen, plus the closed-up house, plus
the old lap-dog, give her, yes, a musty stink
but put a beribboned toddler on her knee—and *voilà!*
she just smells like Grandma Boots
who will live to be one hundred and can read tea leaves.

Now, take that self-same toddler, howling
as she pukes a Jackson Pollock in her crib,
and tell her Papa (who picks her up, wipes the putrid
mess from her hair, then carries her
to his own bed to sleep out the morning) that she stinks.

He knows, but what would he do
without it?
What, without the funk of cottage cheese
in a teacup on the bedstand?
Without the scumjum
of the parents' sheets?

Stink tells us we are fed, we are family, there is plenty,
and the worst our bodies can do
will not drive away
that blind, mute, stupid drive
to come close, sniff
and breathe us in.

■ February

I missed the snow in a winter of snows.
Inside, while ice made a crystalline shell of my house,
I nursed babies and tended the fire.

I would have missed the flood, but it came to us—
swelling upward, pounding down. With sudden thirst,
the river lapped the road. And again

night rises in a dream of drowning.
Water. The stomach of sadness,
the something in a bathtub too tender to touch.

My daughter was alive and running through the house,
chattering as she does about those who must sleep
and what they may have for dinner—

she had just passed when I entered the bathroom
to find another Isabelle (not a real girl at all)
there in the tub, her face a foot under water.

My husband came in and spoke of the day.
Straightening the soap dish, he reached down to lug
the false weight of her out, and then as if

she were something to clean, handed her to me.
Briefly, she sputtered and her eyes
splashed backwards, ruined—but of course

this was not Isabelle, not anyone at all.
I already had so many children.
How could I possibly mother this broken girl?

From the bathroom window I saw a mountain
not there the day before,
newborn with a crooked spine,

then woke to rain upon rain,
my true daughter's hand
tucked in the sleeve of my gown

where she'd found it, silent, in the night.

■ My Sister the Buddhist Prays with the Fleas

She imagines beside her five thousand spirit fleas
fanning out in the endless ellipses of the dead;
a tiny Buddha of Compassion floats above each flea-soul,
ushering them onward with his complicated arms.
Oh Heruka, guide these poor fleas to wherever they're going
—to the Buddha of the Future, the Buddha
of next Tuesday when our rugs are sucked clean
and the cats lick their prickled underbellies
with elaborate care, and the dog like a doormat dreams
all afternoon without scratching, without even wondering
why he is not scratching. Meaning, I guess, *forgive me....*
And, *let all this be about something*
other than suffering or math.

Yet the rich nursing home owner who took an ax
to his new wife's locked bedroom door—
yelling (they have it on tape) "I'm going to bash your fucking face in!
I'm going to crush you, crush you, Anne, and love it!"—
was surely not thinking of the great equilibrium in loving,
how Attachment and Release are weary twins
on either end of a see-saw, mocking one another
as they ride.   And the wife, having broken
both ankles and a wrist from her
two-story jump out the window,
did not smile when asked if she was happy
with the million-dollar settlement, but simply stated,
"Happy? The bastard should be in jail."

Meanwhile somewhere, kudzu overtakes a road bank,
covering what we've planted in our own histories—
in that other life—when I was a chick
scraping in the dirt yard,
and my sister, the boy who scattered corn before me.
As I scurried from the shed to peck
kernels off his boots, he never flinched or kicked
—and when the family finally ate me,
the boy was the one to speak the blessing at the table.

We can't return. Still,
sometimes wetness glistens
like early morning in my feathers.
I almost hear him call me from his back porch stoop.

■ Cupboard

I went there seeking something to pour water into
and found that I was something to pour water into.

I went there seeking tiny grains and seed.
Blackbirds were wintering in my head
and I had to feed them.

We only need one cupboard, don't we?
We could keep it empty and closed most of the time.

It is white of course and if there were a war
we could unhinge its door and carry it into the fields
as a kind of shield.

In times of peace, we would open and close it,
whispering new words inside.

Then perhaps the word itself
could find a way
to protect us.

the end of everything

The end of everything is in the beginnings for me.

The Naked and the Dead
Norman Mailer

■ Toaster Genesis

In the beginning there was a toaster that dreamed of swallowing
a mango pit.

In the beginning there was a mango pit that couldn't keep the hair
out of its eyes.

In the beginning I was laid down on a cold asbestos floor, a bright
coin also on the floor,
almost within reach.

We didn't know in the beginning what not to name each other.

In the beginning,   1) why girls must hurl their flat chests
against the box of understanding;
2) why boys must shudder and release
like an old fashioned camera;
3) the idea of balloon rockets but never
the rockets themselves.

I have read enough to know there was never a beginning
except this:

something not light,
something light,

an eyelash flicking wind,

lips opening
to spill out sky.

There was a bone and inside the bone, not marrow,
but thirst

and so there was water.

There was dirt,
and beneath the dirt,
heat of another hand.

■ A Novel About a Glass of Water

Yes, I know it's water.

I am trying to return to some quiet place,
the way birds and bears return.

How could I write a novel about passionate rumblings in the
    teepees?
Or goldminers who strike up a deal with a nun?

I'm no nun,
though I keep ending up
in the correspondence of people who know me
surrounded by words like "domestic" and "please."

Something else is still possible:
the mind roaring dream-ward, perhaps,
a bowl glazed with green?

As a girl, I kept seamonkeys for company and
voted for Jimmy Carter in my class's mock election.
Nothing then prepared me
for how sack-like a body could get—
the dreg of muscle required to haul its soul
from one chair to another.

Let me tell you
            a fable instead:

    The water was clear and cold and safe to drink; there was
        plenty for everyone.
    The water adored the priest and the priest, likewise.
    He would dip his hands in the well and shudder like a sack
        full of bees.

    The water said to the priest, *It's not that things happen at
        the right time.*
    They just happen, so you might as well believe they were
    right.

The priest answered, *I have a friend*
who believes we ought to put everyone with AIDS
on an island somewhere and let them fight it out.

The priest knew nothing of romance, but everything of love.
Shut your eyes,
               the water responded,
                             put your mouth next to me.

■ Finding Good

You'll find some
in a selfish cat
(perhaps the sweet whorled ear

where the Mama's petting voice
curls itself to sleep
"oh precious, precious one").

You'll find some in the sky
and the slips of wavering air
that do not seem quite to be sky.

You'll find weakness
in many of us
and that is also good

for the weak do not care
how they love—shameless, they
gnash their teeth and howl.

You'll find some.
You'll find some.
So at last

what good you find
may be balled together
like scraps of leftover foil

and after a while there might be enough
for people to stop by the roadside.
To stop and photograph it.

■ Certain Homes in Certain Towns at the End of the World

There is a room where the house cricket
has her own small desk and a tidy, open notebook.

She is welcome to sit there all day if she likes,
not humming, not writing a word.

There are similar rooms
for the flies.

Rooms for the field mice come in from the fields.
Rooms for the moths, rooms for the lice.

A single bookshelf holds whole colonies of vermin.
A single windowsill, a million lives.

In this house, the cat settles on the sofa
and strokes his own ears.

His fleas. His fleas' remembrances.
Ah, his fleas' regrets.

■ The Museum of Weightlessness

Here, I can stroll entire blocks with nothing in my hands.
No purse, no keys,
                    no still-life oranges.
                              I go
clean as bleach. I go
                the way of the bustle,
subtle torture, mustard plasters, ghosts
—into previous centuries.

Has anyone ever told you your life
is a museum?

I am, for the moment, a cityscape in oil: the sunset
melts my lungs.
                      Don't ask me to heal the sick, feed the poor,
I trek instead all day through these pink streets.

Come closer, now, and frame me: note the dove above my shoulder;
my skin, the exaggerated texture of a well-cooked lima bean.

At the next turn, it goes all gray and black (bold strokes)
   harlot yellow.
There were other choices, but I prefer
this mantra of color—a meditation
defined by the objects in the meditation room,
a museum of weightlessness where june bugs like electrons
orbit me.

A caption reads: *The artist's use of paradox and longing....*

Fill your mouth with it.

■ Poem for What Has Come

There was the time I waited.
There was the time you came.
There was much stomach-sadness for a friend's afflicted newborn
and the wish for something else, and such talk of something else
it left us weak, but there was nothing else.

There were clay pigeons loosed in my mind, the gunfire certainty
that the shot would come and shatter.

What was not but should have been a moon
murmured in my ear, "Mary, your child
is tied by ribbon to the Lord's chest.
Do you want her? Should we cut her loose?"

And what was I to say? "Come on, then."

There was the time I trembled like the anger on a lip
taut and full of feeling before speech. But I was not angry
and in the end I said nothing.

There were so many times. We were such children then.

■ Notes

"The Fat Cat" borrows from an interpretation of the Danish "fat cat" folktale by Jack Kent.

Thanks to Susan Eder, whose images of cloud letters inspired "The Photographer."

The title and first lines of "Oh the Dreadful" refer to a Scottish ballad in which a fiddler turns the body of a drowned woman into a violin.

Several ideas from "I Ching" are taken from *The I Ching Workbook* by R.L. Wing.

■ The Autumn House Poetry Series

Michael Simms, Executive Editor

Snow White Horses, Selected Poems 1973–88 by Ed Ochester
The Leaving, New and Selected Poems by Sue Ellen Thompson
Dirt by Jo McDougall
Fire in the Orchard by Gary Margolis
Just Once, New and Previous Poems by Samuel Hazo
The White Calf Kicks by Deborah Slicer ● 2003, selected by
   Naomi Shihab Nye
The Divine Salt by Peter Blair
The Dark Takes Aim by Julie Suk
Satisfied with Havoc by Jo McDougall
Half Lives by Richard Jackson
Not God After All by Gerald Stern, with drawings by Sheba Sharrow
Dear Good Naked Morning by Ruth L. Schwartz ● 2004, selected by
   Alicia Ostriker
A Flight to Elsewhere by Samuel Hazo
Collected Poems by Patricia Dobler
The Autumn House Anthology of Contemporary American Poetry
   edited by Sue Ellen Thompson
Déjà Vu Diner by Leonard Gontarek
lucky wreck by Ada Limon ● 2005, selected by Jean Valentine

The Golden Hour by Sue Ellen Thompson
Woman in the Painting by Andrea Hollander Budy
Joyful Noise: An Anthology of American Spiritual Poetry
   edited by Robert Strong
No Sweeter Fat by Nancy Pagh ● 2006, selected by Tim Seibles
Unreconstructed: Poems Selected and New by Ed Ochester
Rabbis of the Air by Philip Terman
Let It Be a Dark Roux: New and Selected Poems by Sheryl St. Germain
Dixmont by Rick Campbell
The River Is Rising by Patricia Jabbeh Wesley
The Dark Opens by Miriam Levine ● 2007, selected by Mark Doty
The Song of the Horse by Samuel Hazo
My Life as a Doll by Elizabeth Kirschner
She Heads into the Wilderness by Anne Marie Macari
When She Named Fire: An Anthology of Contemporary Poetry by
   American Women edited by Andrea Hollander Budy
67 Mogul Miniatures by Raza Ali Hasan
A Theory of Everything by Mary Crockett Hill ● 2008, selected by
   Naomi Shihab Nye

● winner of the annual Autumn House Press Poetry Prize

■ Design and Production

Cover and text design by Kathy Boykowycz

Text set in Lucida Sans, designed in 1085 by Charles Bigelow
and Kris Holmes

Printed by Thomson-Shore Inc. of Dexter, Michigan, on Natures
Natural, a 30% recycled paper